BYRON KATIE

on

Self-Realization

Edited by Stephen Mitchell

the work of
byron katie
WWW.THEWORK.COM

BYRON KATIE INTERNATIONAL, INC. • LOS ANGELES

Originally published in 2000 as *A Brief Anthology of Katie's Words*.

Published in the United States by:
Byron Katie International, Inc.
578 Washington Blvd. Box 821
Marina del Rey, CA 90292
1-800-98KATIE (52843)
www.thework.com

ISBN 1-890246-82-4

Printed in the United States of America.
Design & Layout by Balsam Design
Art Director: Richard Balsam
Production Specialist: Emily Eoff
Cover Photography: Brie Childers

To Paula Brittain,
Melony Malouf,
Mischelle Miller,
Lesley Pollitt,
to Bob Brittain and to Penfield Chester,
with love and gratitude

The Work of Byron Katie:
The Four Questions and Turnaround

1. Is it true?
2. Can you absolutely know that it's true?
3. How do you react when you believe that thought?
4. Who would you be without the thought? *and*

Turn it around.

Life on the other side of inquiry is so simple
and obvious that it can't be imagined.
Everything is seen to be at its best, just the
way it is. Hope and faith aren't needed in this
place. Earth turned out to be the heaven I was
longing for. This is the unimaginable life that
I live, that we all live.

As closely as I can describe it in words, I am
your heart. I am what you look like inside
yourself. I am the sweetest place that you
come from. Whether you love me or hate me
depends on whether you love or hate yourself.

I am no one. I am just a mirror. I am the face in the mirror.

As you lose the filter that I call a story, you begin to hear your own self at a higher level, and it starts to sound like me, only in its own way: brilliant, itself. There's a resonance that doesn't ever leave the center. You come to honor it, because you come to realize that you have no authentic life outside it.

I have no ideas about whether you should or shouldn't suffer. I respect your path as much as I respect my own. I understand if you're mesmerized by your story and want to hold on to it. If you say that you *don't* want to suffer, I'm there for you. Through inquiry I'll meet you as deeply as you want to go. Whatever you say, I'll meet it. Whatever you ask for, I'll give. I love you, because I'm totally selfish. Loving you is simply self-love.

My experience is that confusion is the only suffering. Confusion is when you argue with

7

what is. When you're perfectly clear, what is is what you want. So when you want something that's different from what is, you can know that you're very confused.

I am here to take the mystery out of everything. It's simple, because there really isn't anything. There's only the story appearing now. And not even that.

The Work always brings us back to who we really are. Each belief investigated to the point of understanding allows the next belief to surface. You undo that one. Then you undo the next, and the next. And then you find that you are actually looking forward to the next belief. At some point you may notice that you are meeting every thought, feeling, person, and situation as a friend. Until eventually you are looking for a problem. Until, finally, you notice that you haven't had one in years.

Through inquiry, we discover how attachment to a belief or story causes suffering. Before the story there is peace. Then a thought enters, we believe it, and the peace seems to disappear. We notice the feeling of stress in the moment, investigate the story behind it, and realize that it isn't true. The feeling lets us know that we are opposing what is by believing the thought. It tells us that we're at war with reality. When we notice that we're believing a lie and living as if it were true, we become present outside our story. Then the story falls away in the light of awareness, and only the awareness of what really is remains. Peace is who we are without a story, until the next stressful story appears. Eventually inquiry becomes alive in us as the natural, wordless response of awareness to the thoughts and stories that arise.

If you want reality to be different than it is, you might as well try to teach a cat to bark. You can try and try, and in the end the cat will look up at you and say, "Meow." Wanting reality to be different than it is is hopeless. You can spend the rest of your life trying to teach a cat to bark.

I am a lover of what is, not because I'm a spiritual person, but because it hurts when I argue with reality. No thinking in the world can change it. What is is. Everything I need is already here now. How do I know I don't need what I want? I don't have it. So everything I need is supplied.

You can't have an up without a down. You can't have a left without a right. This is duality. If you have a problem, you must already have the solution. The question is, Do you really want the solution, or do you want to perpetuate the problem? The solution is always there. The Work can help you find it. Write down the problem, turn it around, and you have the solution.

I am your heart. I am the depth you don't listen to: in your face, from here. It had to get louder, because your beliefs block it out from there. I am you on the other side of The Work. I am the voice so covered up with beliefs that you can't hear it inside yourself. So I appear out here, in your face—which is really inside yourself.

I don't change, and I only see change in you if you say that there's change. You are my inner life. You're the voice of my self, reporting my health at all times. Sickness or health—it's all fine with me. You're sad, you're not sad; you don't understand, you understand; you're peaceful, you're upset; you're this, you're that. I am each cell reporting itself. And beyond all that, I know that each cell is always at peace.

Fear has only two causes: the thought of losing what you have or the thought of not getting what you want. In either case, the

worst thing that can ever happen is a story.
Nothing you need can be taken from you.
And no one can ever have anything you
need. Need is a story you tell yourself. It is
a lie that causes you pain and separates you
from yourself. It is wanting what is not that
separates you from what is.

A feeling is like the mate to a thought
appearing. It's like a left and a right. If
you have a thought, there's a simultaneous
feeling. And an uncomfortable feeling is
like a compassionate alarm clock that says,

"You're in the dream." It's time to investigate, that's all. But if we don't honor the alarm clock, then we try to alter and manipulate the feeling by reaching into an apparent external world. We're usually aware of the feeling first. That's why I say it's an alarm clock that lets you know you're in a thought that you may want to investigate. If it's not acceptable to you, if it's painful, you might want to inquire and do The Work.

When you are mentally out of your business, you experience immediate separation, loneliness, and fear. If you're lonely or sad, you may ask yourself, "Whose business am I in mentally?" And you may come to see that you've never been present, that you've mentally been living in other people's business all your life. Just to notice that you're in someone else's business can bring you back to your wonderful self. What a sweet place to be. Home.

There are no physical problems—only mental ones.

Depression, pain, and fear are gifts that say, "Sweetheart, take a look at your thinking in this moment. You're living in a story that isn't true for you." Living a lie is always stressful. And investigating a lie through The Work always leads you back to who you are. Who you are is not an option. You are love. It hurts to believe you're other than who you are, to live any story less than love.

I am you. I am so melded into you that when you breathe, it's my breath. When you sit, it's me sitting. You'll say something, and I am absolutely there at that moment. It's as if I own you and you own me. Your voice is my voice, literally. And it doesn't have any meaning for me, so that, without prejudice or separation, I can join it wherever you are.

The reason this speaks is because it does. If I thought *I* was doing it, I wouldn't be such a fool. There's no purpose in my bringing inquiry to people. My only purpose is to do what I'm doing. When I do The Work with someone, my purpose is to sit with that person and ask the questions. If someone asks *me* a question, my purpose is to give my experience through my answer. I'm an effect of their suffering: there's no cause arising here. The cause is what people would call outside me, and their outside is my inside. When someone talks, I'm a listener. When someone asks, I'm a response.

Attachment to a thought means believing that the thought is true. When we don't inquire, we assume that a thought is true, though we can't ever know that. The purpose of attachment is to keep us from the realization that we are already truth. We don't attach to things; we attach to our stories about things.

Thoughts are friends, not enemies. They're just what is. They appear. They're innocent. We're not doing them. They're not personal. They're like the breeze or the leaves on the trees or the raindrops falling. Thoughts arise like that, and we can make friends with them. Would you argue with a raindrop? Raindrops aren't personal, and neither are thoughts. It's the meaning you attach to those thoughts that you think is personal. Inquire. Meet them with understanding. Once a painful concept is met with understanding, the next time it appears you may find it interesting. What used to be the nightmare is now just interesting. The next time it appears, you may find it funny. The next time, you may not even notice it. There will be no attachment. I meet thoughts the way I would meet my children. I meet them with love, gentleness, and a quiet understanding. I inquire.

If you just understand the three kinds of business enough to stay in your own business, it could free your life in a way that you can't even imagine. The next time you're feeling stress or discomfort, ask yourself whose business you're in mentally, and you may burst out laughing! That question can bring you back to yourself. And you may come to see that you've never really been present, that you've been mentally living in other people's business all your life. And if you practice it for a while, you may come to see that *you* don't have any business either and that your life runs perfectly well on its own.

I do The Work with you because you think you need it. I don't have any such thought; I love you just the way you are. That's what I am to myself. You are my internal life. So your asking is my asking. It's just me asking myself for my own freedom. This is self-love. It's perfectly greedy, always.

When someone is facilitating The Work, giving the four questions, he's receiving at another level what I originally received inside me. If he's really doing The Work from a neutral position as he facilitates the four

questions, without any motive, then he's in
the place where I am on the other side. It just
gains in its freedom. It's in or out: unlimited.

Wherever you come from, I'll come from that
same position in order to meet you. That's
why there appears to be a contradiction
between some of the things I say. I'm coming
from different directions, and they're all
true. Every vantage point is equal. It can
sound like a direct retraction or like a puppy
chasing its tail: it seems to go nowhere. It can
sound like someone speaking in riddles. It

can be confusing, and from one vantage point it can't be followed. One of the wonderful things about The Work is that I can be talking with someone and he won't hear the paradox because we are so intimately joined, whereas to someone in the audience it may sound like gibberish. But if you are listening without thinking about what I mean and just letting yourself bathe in the experience of it, going inside and answering the questions for yourself, rather than waiting for the person in the chair to answer, you won't hear it as gibberish. It will make perfect sense.

People often ask me if I'm an enlightened being. I don't know anything about that. I am just someone who knows the difference between *this hurts* and *this doesn't*. I am someone who only wants what is. To meet as a friend each concept that arose turned out to be my freedom. That's where The Work begins and ends—in me. The Work says, "Love it all, exactly as it is." And it shows you how. Wisdom is simply knowing the difference between what hurts and what doesn't hurt. There's immense freedom in that. It doesn't mean you have to do the right thing. It just allows you to stop fooling yourself and do what you do with some awareness. One way leads to suffering; the other way leads to peace.

The world is your perception of it. Inside and outside always match—they are reflections of each other. The world is the mirror image of your mind. If you experience chaos and confusion inside, your external world has to reflect that. You have to see what you believe, because you are the confused thinker looking out and seeing yourself. You are the interpreter of everything, and if you're chaotic, what you hear and see has to be chaos. Even if Jesus, even if the Buddha, were standing in front of you, you would hear confused words, because confusion would be the listener. You would only hear what you thought he was saying, and you'd start arguing with him the first time your story was threatened.

God's will and my will are the same, whether I notice it or not.

To think that we know what's best for another person is to be out of our business. The result is worry, anxiety, and fear. When we mentally step out of our business, we think that we know more than he, she, or God. The only real question is "Can we know what's right for ourselves?" That is our only business. And, as we eventually come to see, not even that.

What I love about The Work is that we come to see that both states—what you call bliss and what you call ordinary—are equal. One is not a higher state than another. There's nothing to strive for anymore, nothing to leave behind. That's the beauty of inquiry—it doesn't matter where we are, it's all good.

Teacher is not a word that I would use to describe myself, though I respect it. You ask me a question, and I answer you, and you hear what you think I say, and you set yourself free. I am your projection. I am, for you, no more and no less than your story of me. You tell the story of how I'm wonderful or how I'm terrible. You see me as an enlightened being and make me into an all-knowing guru

and fairy godmother, or you see me as a New
Age spiritual flake, or you see me as a friend.
What I want is for you to see me the way you
see me. That's where the value is. You will
give me to yourself, or you will take me from
yourself. I just want what you want.

Teacher implies that we all don't teach equally
or have equal wisdom. And that's not true.
Everyone has equal wisdom. It is absolutely
equally distributed. No one is wiser than
anyone else. There's no one who can teach
you except yourself.

The privilege of not having a teacher is
that there's no tradition, so there's nothing
to attach to. This one doesn't have to look
like anything but what it is. It's just such a
fool—it doesn't know anything but love. It's
God delighted. It comes to take the mystery
and importance out of everything. It takes the
push and the time out of it.

You can't make a wrong decision; you can
only experience the story arising about how
you did it. I like to ask, "Are you breathing
yourself?" No? Well, maybe you're not

thinking yourself or making decisions either.
Maybe it doesn't move until it moves, like a
breath, like the wind. And you tell the story
of how you are doing it to keep yourself from
the awareness that you are nature, flowing
perfectly. Who would you be without the story
that you need to make a decision? If it's your
integrity to make a decision, make it. And
guess what? In five minutes, you might change
your mind and call it "you" again.

I like speaking from the earth place. I like
what I call my disguise. The first thing I did

on awakening was to fall in love with form. I
fell in love with the eyes and the floor and the
ceiling. I am that. I am that. I am that. It's
nothing, and it's everything. I love earth. I love
the body of me. None of it is separate. Just to
be born into it with eyes open is enough. Just
to be born, now, into this goodness.

Whenever you invite me, I'll jump into your
dream. I don't have a reason why I shouldn't.
I'll follow you through the tunnel, into the
darkness, into the pit of hell. I'll go there,
and I'll take you by the hand, and we'll walk

through it together into the light. There's no place I won't go. I'm everything, everywhere. It's all a dream. I'll show you. That's what's so sweet about the four questions—they don't care what the story is. They just wait to be asked. They just wait for you to ask them.

It's common for me to speak from the position of a personality, from the position of mankind, from the position of the earth, from the position of God, from the position of a rock. And I'll call myself "it," because I don't have a reference point for separation.

I am all those things, and I don't have any
concept that I'm not. I've simply learned to
speak in a way that doesn't alienate people.
It leaves me as benign, unseen, unknown. It
leaves me as a comfortable place for people. I
speak to them from the position of a friend,
and people trust me because I meet them
wherever they are. How do I do that? I'm in
love. I'm in passionate, blissful love. It's a love
affair with itself. To meet people where they
are, without any conditions, is to meet my
own self without conditions. It's the simplest
thing in the world. I'm always intoxicated with
this love affair. I'm in love with everything.
It's total vanity. I would kiss the ground I

walk on—it's all me. But to kiss the ground would draw attention to itself. That's what the first three years looked like. It's subtler now, more invisible. It has matured.

Decisions are easy. It's the story you tell about them that isn't easy. When you jump out of a plane and you pull the parachute cord and it doesn't open, you feel fear, because you have the next cord to pull. So you pull that one and it doesn't open. And that's the last cord. Now there's no decision to make. No decision, no fear, so just enjoy the trip! And that's my position—I'm a lover of what is. What is: no cord to pull. It's already happening. Free fall. I have nothing to do with it.

I'm a lover of reality, because I know the freedom and power of being that lover. All I want is what is. That's it. My plan to change things could only leave me with less. Even a simple thought like "I'm not okay" can be depressing, because it's a flat-out lie. Even on my deathbed, I'm okay. That is the truth.

My own experience is that I live in completeness, and that all of us do. It is the peace I walk in. I don't know anything. I don't have to figure anything out. I gave up forty-three years of thinking that went nowhere, and now I can be in the Don't-know. This leaves nothing but peace and joy in my life. It's the absolute fulfillment of watching everything unfold in front of me as me.

Any story that you tell about yourself causes suffering. There is no authentic story.

What is God's intention? Whose business is God's intention? To go mentally into God's business is to be immediately lonely. That is why I keep that solid center—God is good, God is everything. I know his intention; it's exactly what is in every moment. In fact, "God" is another name for what is. I don't have to question it anymore; it's over. I don't have to be outside myself, meddling in God's business. It's simple. God is good, God is everything. And from that basis it's clear that everything is perfect. Then, if we investigate, we lose even that. And that is intimacy. That is God itself. One with. One as. Itself.

It's not your job to like me—it's mine.

The four questions unraveled each story, and the turnaround led back to the storyteller— me. I am the storyteller. I become the story I tell myself. And I am what lives prior to every story. Every story, every thing is God: reality. It apparently emerges from out of Itself, and appears as a life. It lives forever within the story, until the story ends. From out of Itself I appeared as my story, until the questions brought me home. I love it that inquiry is so unfailing. Story; pain; investigation; no story.

Freedom is possible in every moment. This is The Work, the great undoing.

I stand as an untapped resource. What I'm here for is to bring this anti-virus that I call The Work to those who think it would serve them. It's not for everyone. It's just an offering. That's what can be of use. Not my words, not my presence, nothing about me is of value. What is of value can't be seen or heard. I'm invisible. But what is manifest are the four questions and the turnaround. That is where the value is. That's what can be experienced when people are tired of suffering. They can reach out and have that, because it is their very own. Whenever it seems personal, as if I'm the one who has it, no one can accept it, because there is nothing personal, and they know this deep inside. They can take the questions and find themselves. The questions are the path back to our self. That's where I can be understood. I am you in the answers. At the center, that's where we meet. It's the only way I can be seen, heard, or understood: at the center, the heart, the truth. I'm only born to people there.

When you love what is, it becomes so simple to live in the world. The world is exactly as it should be. Everything is God. Everything is good. We're always going to get what we need, not what we think we need. Then we come to see that what we need is not only what we have, it's what we want. Then we come to want only what is. That way we always win, no matter what.

My experience is that I'm free. It's how I live internally. I have investigated my thinking, and I've discovered that it doesn't mean a thing. I shine with the joy of understanding. I know about suffering, and I know about joy, and I know who I am. I am goodness. That is who we all are. There's no harm here. I would extinguish myself before I would step on an ant intentionally, because I know how to live. With no story, there's nothing to worry about. When there is nothing to do, nowhere to go, no one to be, no past or future, everything feels right. It's all good.

What does compassion look like? At a funeral, just eat the cake! You don't have to know what to do. It's revealed to you. Someone will come into your arms. It speaks. You're not doing it. Compassion is not a doing. Don't bother thinking about it; just eat the cake. If you're connected through pain, you're just standing or you're sitting. And if there's no pain, you're still just standing or sitting. But one way you're comfortable, the other way you're not.

Only in this moment (which doesn't exist) are we in reality. Everyone can learn to live in the moment, *as* the moment, to love what is in front of you, to love it as you. The miracle of love comes to you in the presence of the uninterpreted moment. If you are mentally somewhere else, you miss real life.

I experience everything in slow motion. More accurately, I experience everything frame by frame by frame. It's like looking at the comics in the newspaper. You see this frame saying this and the next frame saying that. Each word is a frame for me. Each moment is a frame. Each frame is a universe in itself, not connected with any other. It's everything in itself. It's like the rock with lichen on it that you look at through a magnifying glass: a universe in itself, completely undivided. When I'm walking, each movement within one step is complete in itself. It's one step at a time, but actually it's everything in between that too. Now. Now. Now. Now. There is literally no time and space, no past or future or present even, no one coming, no one going. It's just this, as it is—now. There's no meaning to it, no motive in it. And finally you get to a place where nothing moves. That is home, the place we all long for, the still point, the center of the universe, absolute zero.

❧

When something's over, it's over. We all know when that point comes, and we can honor it or ignore it. When my hand reaches out for a cup of tea, I lavish myself on the whole cup of tea, though I don't know if I'm going to finish one sip, three sips, ten sips, or the whole cup. Someone gave me a precious gift the other day, and I loved it. But the gift was in the receiving. In that it was over, and I noticed that I gave it away immediately. Its purpose was over. There's no value to even the most precious object beyond the giving and receiving.

There's such abundance here, now, always.
There's a table. There's a floor. There's a rug
on the floor. There's a window. There's a sky. A
sky! There are two friends—not one, not zero,
but two. I could go on and on describing the
world I live in now. It would take a lifetime to
describe this moment, this now, which doesn't
even exist except as my story. And isn't it
beautiful? Reality as it is. It just is. I could die
in such abundance, and I didn't do anything
for it but notice.

We buy a home for our children, for our bodies; we get a garage for our car; we have doghouses for our dogs; but we won't give the mind a home. And we treat it like an outcast. We shame it and blame it and shame it again. But if you let the mind ask its questions, then the heart will rise with the answer. And "rising" is just a metaphor. The heart will reveal the answer, and the mind can finally rest at home in the heart and come to see that it and the heart are one. That's what these four questions are about. You write down the problem and investigate, and the heart gives you the answer you've always known. Now notice the turnaround to yourself. This is humility. There's nothing else to do. Standing in a room, or sitting in a chair, just watch the story. If it's frightening or depressing, ask four questions, turn it around. Come home.

Just let it be. You may as well; it is. Everything moves in and out at its own time. You have no control. You never have; you never will. You only tell the story of what you think is happening. Do you think you cause movement? You don't. It just apparently is, but you tell the story of how you had something to do with it. "I moved my legs. I

decided to walk." I don't think so—inquire
and see that it's just a story about what is. You
know that you are going to move because
everything is happening simultaneously. You
tell the story before the movement, because
you already are that. *It* moves, and you think
that you did it. Then you tell the story of how
you're going somewhere or how you're doing
something. The only place you can play with
is the story. That's the only game in town.
It's a beginning.

Some people think that compassion means
feeling another person's pain. That's nonsense.
It's not possible to feel another person's pain.
You imagine what you'd feel if you were in
that person's shoes, and you feel your own
projection. Who would you be without your
story? Pain-free, happy, and totally available
if someone needs you—a listener, a teacher
in the house, a Buddha in the house, the one
who lives it. As long as you think there's a you
and a me, let's get the bodies straight. What
I love about separate bodies is that when you
hurt, I don't—it's not my turn. And when
I hurt, you don't. Can you be there for me
without putting your own suffering between

us? Your suffering can't show me the way. Suffering can only teach suffering.

Without a teacher there was no one to tell me that thought was an enemy. So it was only natural that eventually I would meet each thought arising and welcome it as a friend. I can't meet you as an enemy and not feel it. So how could I meet a thought within me as an enemy and not feel it? When I learned to meet my thinking as a friend, I noticed that I met every human as a friend. Because what could you say that has not appeared within me as a thought? It's so simple.

There's no suffering in the world; there's only an uninvestigated story that leads you to believe it. There's no suffering in the world that's real. Isn't that amazing! Investigate and come to know it for yourself.

We only fear what we are—what we haven't gone inside and taken a look at and met with understanding. If I think you might see me as boring, it would frighten me, because I haven't investigated that thought. So it's not people that frighten me, it's me that frightens me. That's my job, to frighten me, until I investigate and stop this fear for myself. The worst that can happen is that I think you think about me what I think about myself. So I am sitting in a pool of me.

When you become a lover of what is, the war is over. No more decisions to make. I like to say, "I'm a woman with no future." No decisions to make, no future. All my decisions are made for me, as they're all made for you. You're just mentally telling the story of how you have something to do with it.

Until there's peace within you, there is no peace in the world, because you are the world, you are the earth. The story of earth is all there is of earth and beyond. When you're in dreamless sleep at night, is there a world? Not until you open your eyes and say "I." "I woke up." "I have to go to work." "I'm going to brush my teeth." Until "I" is born, no world. When the I arises, welcome to the movie of who you think you are. Get the popcorn, here it comes! If you investigate it, and the I arises, there's no attachment. It's just a great movie. And if you haven't investigated, the I arises, it's body-identified, you think it's real, you think there's an "I." Pure fantasy. And if you attach to it, if you think you're that, you may want to inquire.

We do only three things: we stand, we sit, and we lie horizontal. When you're successful, you'll still be sitting somewhere. You'll still be lying down on something. You have to lie down *somewhere*—here is good! What is success? You want the three-thousand-dollar chair, not the ninety-nine-dollar one? Well, sitting is sitting. Even when we're sitting, it's our story about where, what, how. Without a story, I'm successful wherever I am. I know how to stand, sit, and lie down.

I am very clear that the whole world loves me. I just don't expect everyone to be aware of it yet.

You can't have it, because you already *are* it. You already have what you want. You already are what you want. This is as good as it gets. It appears as this now. Perfect. Flawless. And to argue with that is to experience the lie. The Work can give you this wonderful awareness: the awareness of the lie and the power of truth. The beauty of what really is.

Don't pretend yourself beyond your evolution.

You don't experience anxiety unless you've attached to a thought that isn't true for you. It's that simple. You don't ever feel anxiety until you believe that a thought is true, and it's not.

There is a sweetness about the earth. I call it reality. Someone once referred to me as the master of descension. He said, "I've heard of masters of ascension, but you are the master of descension." So, because I had no teacher, reality sounds like this: fall in love with what is. Woman sitting in chair with cup of tea.

That's as sweet as I want it, because that is what is. When you love what is, it becomes so simple to live in the world. The world is exactly as it should be. Everything is God. Everything is good.

We are really alive when we live in non-belief—open, waiting, trusting, and loving to do what appears in front of us now.

People talk about self-realization, and this is it! Can you just breathe in and out? To hell with enlightenment! Just enlighten yourself in this moment. Can you just do that? And then, eventually, it all collapses. The mind finds a home in the heart. The mind merges with the heart and comes to see that it's not separate. It finds a home and it rests. It can't be threatened or scolded or frightened away. Until the story is met with understanding, there is no peace. Only love and understanding heal.

Mind appears to flow everywhere, but it is the unmoving, the never-having-moved. The only flow is awareness. It appears as everything. Eventually, it sees that nowhere is where it is. Its unceasing work is self-realization. It feels humble, because it sees that what hasn't been created can't be claimed. It's left in a state of gratitude for everything: for itself.

The ego is terrified of the truth. And the truth is that the ego doesn't exist.

The Work always leaves you with less of a
story. Who would you be without your story?
You never know until you inquire. There is no
story that is you or that leads to you. Every
story leads away from you. Turn it around;
undo it. You are what exists before all stories.
You are what remains when the story is
understood.

Someone says, "Oh, it's a terrible day; I'm so
depressed." He is the champion of suffering,
saying that there's something wrong here,
something less than beauty. It's the mirror

image without a clue that it's just a mirror image. Just be the is, the storyless movement, the reflection—nothing more. And in that, the source is known and merged. The reflection moves without argument as God. And that is awareness, the joy of what people call the world and what I refer to as the image of God Itself dancing. Even the story of a problem, when it is investigated, is laughable. Even that is God.

Do you want to meet the love of your life? Look in the mirror.

I'll say things like, "Until I'm free to be happy in the presence of my worst enemy, my work's not done." And people can hear that as a motive for doing The Work. It's not—it's an observation. If you do The Work with some kind of motive—of getting your wife back or getting sober—forget it! Do The Work for the love of truth, for the love of freedom. Isn't that what you want your wife for anyway? So that you can be happy and free? Well, skip that, and be happy and free now! You're it. You're the one. There's nothing else to do.

People ask how I can live if nothing has any
meaning and I'm no one. It's very simple. We
are being lived. We're not doing it. Are you
breathing yourself? That's the end of the story.
Did *you* just put your hand on your face? Did
you plan it? Without a story, we move quite
well. Effortlessly. In perfect health. Fluidly,
freely, with a lot of love. And without war,
without resistance. This possibility can be
very frightening for people who think that
they have control. So investigate, and see how
life goes on, so much more joyfully. Even in
its apparent collapsing, I see only joy.

If you knew how important you were—and without the story you come to know it—you would fragment into a billion pieces, and just be light. That's what these misunderstood concepts are for, to keep you from the awareness of that. The appearance of love, that's who you'd have to be if you knew it— just a fool, blind with love. It takes so much pain to live out of the light. I don't know how people do it for so long. It was so painful that I could only do it for forty-three years. Forty-three centuries.

Your ego has to terrify you all the time, so
that you can investigate and come home
to yourself in the body. This is what we are
all here to live. When we aren't attached
to our thinking, when all the why's, when's,
and where's let go of us, then what really is
becomes visible.

The fear of death is the last smokescreen
for the fear of love. The mind looks at
nothing and calls it something, to keep from
experiencing what it really is. Every fear is
the fear of love, because to discover the truth

of anything is to discover that there is nobody, no doer, no me to create suffering or to identify with anything. And so, without any of that, there is just love.

Self meeting itself—that's the deal. If I wait for God to enlighten me, it's not so easy. It can be a long wait—years, decades maybe. When I'm on my knees praying to God in all sincerity, *I'm* the one listening. Can I do what I've begged God to do? Can I hear myself? Who else is listening? I'm a lover of reality. Can I just listen to myself? And when I hear

myself, there's no separation. If I want God
to do it, I turn it around. And in the peace of
that, I come to know the truth.

Live in the Now? Even the thought "Now"
is a concept. Before the thought completes
itself, it's gone, with no proof that it ever
existed. Even thought doesn't exist. That's
why everyone already has the quiet mind that
they're seeking.

All pleasure is pain, until I understand. Then I am the pleasure I was seeking. I am what I always wanted. Pleasure is a mirror image of what we already have before we look away from what really is. When we stop seeking pleasure, the beauty concealed by the seeking becomes evident. It's so simple and clear. What we wanted to find from pleasure is simply what is left beyond all stories.

There is no beginning of time, only beginning of thought.

The illusion is the mirror image attaching to a concept or belief. The illusion is the ego thinking that it's separate. It's not. It goes where God goes. God—reality—is all of it. The ego has no options. It can protest all it wants, but if God moves, *it* moves.

To me, reality is God, because it rules. How do I know that my brother should have died? He did. That's reality. That's what is. It doesn't wait for my vote or my opinion. And even that doesn't exist, because what is is the story of a past. What I love most about a story of the past is that it's over. That's why I'm a lover of reality. It's always kinder than the story.

The voice within is what I honor. It's what I'm married to. This life doesn't belong to me. The voice says, "Brush your teeth." Okay. I don't know what for, I just move on through. It says, "Walk." Okay. I just keep moving. Someone says, "Will you come do The Work with us?" Okay. I'm just following orders. The beautiful thing about this is that it's fun. If I don't follow the order, it's okay too. This is a game about where it will take me if I do follow. For forty-three years I was at war out in the story. And then one day, in a moment of clarity, I found my way back home. And that's what we're doing here—inquiry. It comes out from source and it returns to source. It's such a gift. I was always merging into my stories, into my insanity. And then, one day, when I heard "Brush your teeth," it started coming back, and there was a receiver. And it opened, like a womb. It opened into that allowing, into the mystery. Each moment—new! "Brush your teeth." It doesn't sound very spiritual to me, but that's all it said. "Walk." It just opens and it becomes more of a listener. All marriage is nothing more than a metaphor of that marriage. And if I don't follow, if I tell it, "Later," I don't feel very comfortable. And then I come back and I brush my teeth. It becomes a thing that's timeless, because when you're opening to that, there's no time and space in it. It's just a "Yes. Yes. Yes." That's why I say, "Boundaries are an act of selfishness." I don't have any. When it says, "Jump," I jump. Because where I jump, I have nothing to lose. There's nothing more fun than following such an insane thing and saying "Yes" to it. You don't have anything to lose. You're dead already. You can afford to be a fool.

Every word is the sound of God. Every word is the word of God. There is nothing personal here. And everything is personal. If the moon rises, it's for you. You're the one watching it! (And that's just a beginning.)

The litmus test for self-realization is the constant state of gratitude. That's the energy. This gratitude is not something a person can look for or find. It comes from another direction. It takes us over completely. It's so vast that it can't be dimmed or overlaid with anything that could hide it. It's like

its own self. The short version would be
God intoxicated with God, Itself. The
total acceptance and consumption of itself
reflected back in the same moment in that
central place that is like fusion—it's the
beginning. What looks like the end is the
beginning. And when you think life is so
good that it can't get any better, it gets better.
It has to. That's a law.

It's personal and it's not personal. It's personal
in that the whole world is me—a mirror
image that I am and love. Without it I'm

bodiless. And it's not that I need to look, it's just that looking is such a delight. On the other hand, it's not personal, because I see nothing more than a mirror image. Until God—reality—moves, I have no movement. Every movement, every sound, every breath, every molecule, every atom is nothing more than a mirror image of God. So I don't move, I'm being moved. I don't do, I'm being done. I don't think, I'm being thought. I don't breathe, I'm being breathed. There is no me, there is nothing personal or real about it. Whenever you speak, it's God speaking. When a flower blooms, it's God. When an army marches, it's God. I see only God. Add one more o and you've got good. To me they're synonymous. How could I not love all that I am, all that you are? One me.

If you find the internal work exciting, you'll come to look forward to the worst that can happen, because you won't find a problem that can't be healed from the inside.
And it becomes a mystery that you ever thought there was a problem—ever. This is paradise found.

Forgiveness is discovering that what you thought happened didn't—that there was never anything to forgive. No one has ever done anything terrible. There is nothing terrible except your thoughts about what you see. So whenever you suffer, inquire, look at the thoughts you're thinking, and set yourself free. Be a child. Know nothing. Take your ignorance all the way to your freedom.

I experience the I arising, and I quake with the privilege of that, because the I is Its very self, being born. When the I arises, It is presenting Itself to Itself. Your name is the name of God. It's equal to "table." "I." "God."

Until we know that death is equal to life, and that it comes in its own sweet way, perfectly, we're going to take on the role of God without the awareness of it, and it's always going to hurt. Whenever you interfere with a process mentally—in the name of life, humanity, anything; in other words, whenever you mentally oppose what is—you're going to experience sadness and apparent separation. There's no sadness without the story. What is is. You *are* it. You're not saving anyone; you're not killing anyone. The world doesn't depend on you.

We're not doing anything. Ultimately, we are being done. If I say, "I'm going to the store," I'm very clear that I am God going to God. *Store* is a word for God. *I* is a word for God. And *God* is a word for what is. When I say I love you, there's no personality talking. It's self-love: I'm only talking to myself. The way I experience it is that It is only talking to Itself. If I say, "Let me pour you some tea", It is pouring Its own tea for Itself, and the tea is Itself. It's so self-absorbed that It leaves no room for any other. Nothing. Not a molecule separate from Itself. That's true love. It's the ultimate self. There's no other existence. It's self-consuming always and loving it. It's a guiltless state. There's no one separate. In the apparent world of duality, people are going to see it as a you and a me, but in reality there is only one. And even that's not true.

Something is better than nothing—is that true? *Something*—a word for God. *Nothing*—

a word for God. The same. There's no preference. Haven't you noticed? Something. Nothing. *God* is a word. We could have used any word. They're all words for God. You attach meaning to a word, and welcome to genesis.

Everything is equal. There is no this soul or that soul. There's only one. And that's the last story. There's only one. And not even that. It doesn't matter how you attempt to be disconnected, it's not a possibility. Any thought you believe is an attempt to break the connection. But it's only an attempt. It can't be done. That's why it feels so uncomfortable.

Even so-called truths eventually fall away. Every truth is a distortion of what is. The last truth—I call it the last judgment—is "God is everything, God is good." Ultimately even this isn't true. But as long as it works for you, I say keep it and have a wonderful life.

We live as awareness, and awareness always focuses on something, because it's everything. It will notice its own finger or foot. Somewhere within it, there's always a focus. Its breath may surf the back of its tongue. It doesn't matter where the awareness is: the breath, the fingers, the toes. Something is going on all the time within it, as it. There's nothing moving it, and yet it's in perpetual motion. Its focus is itself. It is always present, like your heartbeat. It doesn't go faster or slower. It's a steady condition. It's nothing, and it's so beautiful that it wants to call itself something. Now it's a hand on my head, my elbow on the couch, my hands on my foot,

my heart beating, my toes swaying to its
natural rhythm. I notice that my fingers are
doing the same, ever so slightly. It would be
undetectable if I were attached to anything.
And as I speak, the swaying continues. There's
no sound, even though it appears that I'm
talking. When I hear sound, it is silence also.
The tongue hitting the roof of the mouth.
Lips coming together as it speaks. The chair
holding me. Always held. Even in the walking,
the earth holds her.